3 8043 27184177 3

KW-051-716

ECO JOURNEYS

LIFE CYCLE OF A DRINKS CAN

By Louise Nelson

BookLife
PUBLISHING

©2021
BookLife Publishing Ltd.
King's Lynn
Norfolk PE30 4LS
All rights reserved.
Printed in Malta.

A catalogue record for
this book is available
from the British Library.

ISBN: 978-1-83927-858-7

Written by:
Louise Nelson

Edited by:
William Anthony

Designed by:
Dan Scase

Photo credits

Front cover – Littlekidmoment, OlegDoroshin, Chake. Page 4&5 – Akimov Igor, Bauwimauwi. 6&7 – Roman Samokhin, Maksim_Gusev. 8&9 – Ann in the uk, Steve Allen. 10&11 – vchal, Tom Grundy. 12&13 – Rawpixel.com, Artur_eM. 14&15 – siam.pukkato, Paul Vasarhelyi, Cultura Motion, sunsetman, Ian Walsh. 16&17 – Vershinin89, MOLPIX. 18&19 – ppart, kongsky, taviphoto, Kletr, Anton Starikov, Oleksiy Mark, Ieshun irina, Winai Tepsuttinun. 20&21 – uanhuongho, Nichola Chapman, Fadila Suryandika, deannalindsey, elisa galceran garcia. 22&23 – Littlekidmoment, cinarlarinenes, Don Pablo, Maksim_Gusev, Bauwimauwi. Images are courtesy of Shutterstock.com. With thanks to Getty Images, Thinkstock Photo and iStockphoto. All facts, statistics, web addresses and URLs in this book were verified as valid and accurate at time of writing. No responsibility for any changes to external websites or references can be accepted by either the author or publisher.

Contents

Words that look like this can be found in the glossary on page 24.

The Life of a Drinks Can

Lots of people love the pop and fizz of a can of soft drink. When you're out and about, a can is an easy way to grab a drink, and there are lots to choose from.

Drinks cans are made of a metal called aluminium.

Drinks cans are very useful for carrying drinks around. Around 9 <u>billion</u> drinks cans are made in the UK every year.

Do you know what happens to a drinks can when you are finished with it?

What IS Aluminium?

Aluminium is a material. A material is what an object is made of. The properties of a material tell us what it is like. Let's look at the properties of an aluminium can:

- Can be bent and made into shapes
- Can <u>conduct</u> heat
- Not heavy
- Strong
- Smooth
- Shiny

Lots of metals such as aluminium can be found underground, but that does not mean we find metal cans in the earth. Before we can use the aluminium we find, we must <u>melt</u> it.

<u>Liquid</u> metal can be bent and will harden as it cools.

7

The Lifespan of a Drinks can

Drinks cans are made to be used once, then thrown away. This is known as a single-use item. You can't reseal a can and use it for drinks again.

Many families might use hundreds of drinks cans per year.

So what can you do with all these cans? You can't use them again, and you wouldn't want hundreds of empty cans piling up in your house! We can throw cans away, or we can recycle them.

Metal and Mining

If you throw your drinks can in the bin, it will go to a landfill site. Landfill sites are huge pits where we dump our rubbish. They are smelly and bad for the <u>environment</u>.

An aluminium can may stay in a landfill site for hundreds of years.

Drinks cans are sometimes held together with plastic rings. These plastic rings can be very harmful for wildlife if they are put into landfill.

This bird is stuck in a plastic can holder.

What IS Recycling?

You can put your drinks can into a recycling bin instead of a regular bin. This means it will be sent off to be made into something new.

Recycling cans keeps them out of landfill, and saves _energy_.

Empty cans can be recycled into
new cans over and over again!

Recycling is when we turn old, used materials into
new materials. We can collect old aluminium cans
and recycle them into new ones.

Recycling a Drinks can

Once your drinks can is empty, you should rinse it with water to make sure it is clean and not sticky. Look for recycling bins and put your can in the correct one.

Which of these bins is for cans?

PAPER

PLASTIC

CANS

14

If you are at home, you can usually put your can in the recycling bin. It will be collected and taken away for recycling.

Recycling collection

In the park

At school

At a recycling point

15

Aluminium cans at a recycling centre

Aluminium cans go to the recycling centre. At the recycling centre, cans are washed and cut into small pieces.

The small pieces are melted down into new aluminium, ready to use.

16

The recycled aluminium is just as good as new aluminium, but it takes a lot less energy to make. Aluminium can be recycled forever, again and again.

The aluminium is made into new cans.

Trash to Treasure

Most aluminium cans are made into new cans. Aluminium is very <u>versatile</u> and can also be made into other things. Your can could have a new life as:

Aluminium foil

A dishwasher

Food packaging

A <u>reusable</u> bottle

Car parts

Wires

A bike

A ladder

It is much easier to recycle aluminium than dig up new metal and melt it down.

Reuse and Upcycle

A drinks can may only be used once for drinks, but this doesn't mean you have to put it straight in the recycling. Can you reuse your can for something else?

Aluminium is sharp, so always get an adult to help you.

Upcycling means taking something old and used and making it look brand new. With just a little paint and glue, your can will have a new look and a new life.

A mini windmill

Here are some examples of upcycled drinks cans.

A metallic bag

A festive decoration

A pretty flower

21

The Eco Journey of a Drinks Can

The aluminium is ready to be made into something new.

The pieces are melted into bars or thin sheets.

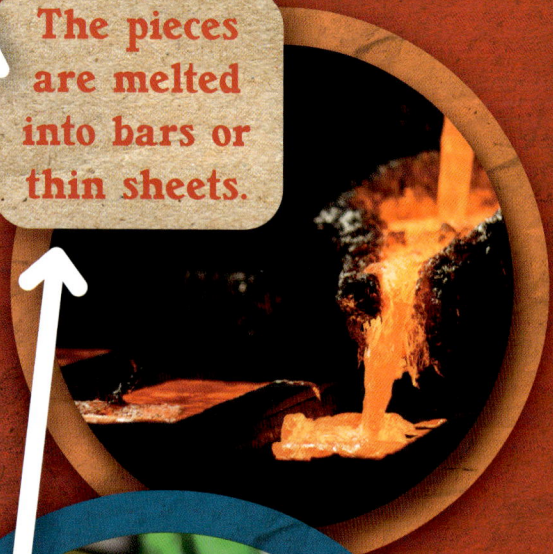

The new can is bought and used.

When it's empty, it should be washed and recycled.

Cans are shredded at the recycling centre.

Quick Quiz

Can you remember the eco journey of a drinks can? Let's see! Look back through the book if you can't remember.

1. What are drinks cans made of?
a) Steel
b) Plastic
c) Aluminium

2. How long does it take for a drinks can to break down in landfill?
a) 1 year
b) Hundreds of years
c) Thousands of years

3. How many times can a drinks can be recycled as another can?
a) Once or twice
b) Forever
c) Drinks cans can't be recycled

4. Which of these is not a property of a drinks can?
a) Smooth
b) Fluffy
c) Shiny

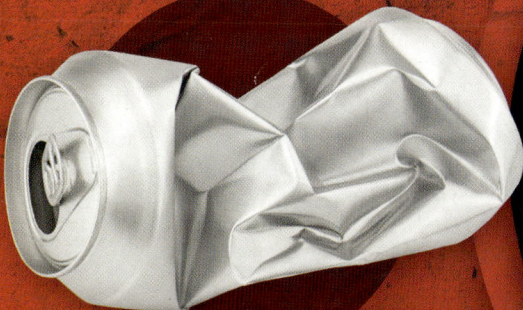

Answers: 1) C, 2) B, 3) B, 4) B

Glossary

billion	one thousand million
conduct	to allow heat or electricity to move from one place to another
energy	a type of power that can be used to do something
environment	the natural world
liquid	a material that flows, such as water
melt	to go runny like water, because of heat
reusable	able to be used again and again
versatile	able to do many different things

Index